8 Keys To Unlocking Your Child's Potential & Development In Sports & Beyond

"There Is A Formula For Success."

By Marcus DiBernardo

About The Author

Coach DiBernardo has 20+ years of soccer coaching and physical education teaching experience. He has spent his entire career teaching and developing athletes from the ages of 4 to 24. Coach DiBernardo also runs a coaching education company with over 30 books and online coaching courses (www.soccersmarttraining.com). His online sports cognitive development course is the first online course of it's kind with the latest cutting edge information and insight into the sports brain.

Coach DiBernardo's desire to coach came early on. His first coaching experience began at the young age of eighteen at his local soccer club in Durham, Connecticut. In the years to come, Coach DiBernardo would go on to lead numerous teams to many titles across the country. In 2011, he was named "National College Coach of The Year". Currently, Coach DiBernardo is the Founder and Director of an International Soccer Academy as well as a Head Men's College Soccer Coach.

Coach DiBernardo possesses a coaching style that is highly team-centric, founded on the principle of mutual respect, hard work and a genuine love for the game of soccer. As a player, he was known for his unwavering commitment and work ethic as defender. Playing at the NCAA Division I level and later moving on to play in the First Division of the CSL, he earned the CCSU College Scholar Athlete Award for soccer in 1993.

Coach DiBernardo holds a number soccer diplomas and licenses. He is a member of the NSCAA Associate National Staff and considers himself a lifetime learner and active student of the game. He strongly believes, the better he can become as a coach, the more rounded the program experience he can design and share with his players.

Introduction

Over the years the number one question I get from the parents of young players is "how can my child improve in the sport"? It is certainly a good question, but it is usually asked when I am walking off the field after training or a game. The reality is for me to answer that question in detail, it could take hours. I decided to write this guidebook in order to help educate parents who really want their child to improve and excel in sports and beyond. Over the past fifteen years there has been a lot of research into how certain people are able to become experts and highly skilled in their particular fields. That research clearly shows there is a formula for success that can be applied to any area in which a person wishes to become skilled. The trick is constructing an age appropriate formula that is fun and uses the most effective coaching & teaching methods. In this book I give you the framework of what it will take in order for your child to become highly skilled and accomplished in the area they choose. The book is also intended to educate parents about what a healthy sports development plan should look like for their child. Parents must be willing to take an active and educated role in their child's development. If you are serious about your child being able to excel and reach their potential, while keeping a healthy balanced lifestyle – this book is for you!

Table of Contents

"8 Keys"

1

Kids Need To Have Fun & Enjoy Their Sport

Key point #1 sounds simple but how often do children get burned out because what they are doing becomes a chore and not fun anymore? Lets take youth soccer in America as an example. Youth soccer in America is the largest participated youth sport in the country, but it also comes with the highest child burnout rate. Why is this the case? In my opinion it all has to do with what we as adults choose to emphasize and deem important. Let me give you a few examples. It is not uncommon in youth soccer today to see U6 competitive leagues and even U8 select travel soccer teams. Is it the kids that wanted these leagues? No. It is the parents who want their child to excel, compete, win and be in first place at the top of the league standings. The parents are emailing the coaches concerned about the performance of their child or their team at 7 years old! Trust me when I tell you, that type of situation is not good for children's sports and their development. There should never be a select team or all-star team at 7 years old! What happens to the kids that didn't make the U7 select team? The players self-esteem is damaged, they think they are not good enough and their confidence levels will most likely dip. It's hard enough to identify elite talent at the age of 16 never mind 7 years old! How can a situation like this be fixed? Let's start with no league play or select teams until U13 (U5-U12 is just all out fun and play). When the players come to the field the coach should "guide them" in a very positive way as they learn the game in a fun and safe training environment. The kids can play games against each other without keeping score or if they keep score there will be rules that stop one team from running away with the score! Example: if a team is winning by 2 goals they will play down a player until the score is tied or some players will switch teams every 10 minutes. The coach should never be a "Dictator", yelling out constant instructions every 5 seconds. The coach should simply set the players up for success and allow them to take charge of their own learning by setting up a training environment that helps the kids learn the game (let the kids make their own choices when training). The practice environment should be a place where players are not afraid to ask questions, not afraid to try new things or make mistakes and where **having fun is the real goal**. The coach's role is really a facilitator or guide for the players learning experience.   Let me be clear about the role of the coach though. I am not saying the coach should not teach the game, teach technique and make some corrections, but after doing this he or she must let the kids play with any fear of making a mistake. The kids should play and enjoy the play as the coach encourages them. The practices can also be arranged so the rules and conditions of the game teach the children, so the coach doesn't have to be as involved all the time. Example: divide the soccer field in half when playing 3v3. Make the rule only 2 players can be in the attacking half of the field at one time. This rule forces the team into a triangle shape with a player always in support back (forming a triangle).   The players may not even realize right away that the rules of the game force them to have proper spacing while establishing good support. This type of practice really allows the coach to be a guide or facilitator and not a "yelling dictator"!

How many times have I sat on the sidelines at many different age levels, being disappointed in the environment that was created by the coaches and parent's. **I can't say this enough for all the parents, encourage your child and the entire group. Tell everyone what a great job they did. That should be your main focus while at the field.** Do not tell the kids where to pass the ball, do not get upset if the team gets scored on and do not yell if a player makes a mistake. In a typical professional game every single player on the field will make multiple mistakes; it is the reality of any sport at any level. Players must be taught it is okay if you make a bad pass or miss a shot. What matters is the reaction of the player. Players need to be taught not get upset or get their head down, simply keep playing hard and having fun. I can't stress enough for children's sports that they must be having fun, learning to work with others, developing emotionally, developing socially and associating playing the sport with a great time. The parents and the coach play a major role in creating the environment the kids will be playing in. It is everyone's responsibility to create a positive fun environment with no pressure. No player should feel bad leaving the field after playing or practicing. The coach is there to help the players ask the right questions (no question is a bad question), guide them in the learning process and offer knowledgeable instruction when needed. Participating in a sport should be a special experience that will boost your child's self-esteem and self-worth while they are having a great time!

#2

Teach Teamwork

I recently heard a great story about a team from Europe who came to the United States to compete in a large soccer tournament in Florida. The European team made the final against a team from Florida. The Florida team had two star players who enjoyed being the stars and always wanted the attention! They would sign autographs before and after the games for the little kids, basking in the spotlight. The final matched the team from Europe against the team from Florida team. The European team ended up beating the team from Florida in the Championship Game rather easily. The European team had the best player in the entire tournament on their team. After the game a couple fans asked the star European player to sign autographs for them. The European player replied, "I am sorry but soccer is a team game and I do not take credit for any of the teams successes by myself, so for that reason I do not sign autographs because that would single me out." I know that is a little bit of an extreme example but the message is such positive message. Whoever was that young persons coach did a great job of teaching the importance of teamwork, humility and respect. This is something that needs to be taught more and more. The "me, me, me" attitude will not help any team or individual develop.

Being part of a team should be an invaluable developmental experience for the player, if the team is run in the right way. The priority of a true team is to always put the team ahead of the individual. Every player is responsible for doing their part to the best of their ability in order to ensure the team will never break down. Players should be encouraged to help each other, offer advice, share ideas and work on techniques together. Creating an environment where players can and want to take responsibility for their learning and the team's progress is very motivating. Players should enjoy coming to training and seeing their teammates. They should feel good about the relationships they are building with their teammates and coaches. Learning and asking questions should never be seen as embarrassing. Every question is a good question because it is a catalyst for learning. This type of environment will make kids confident about the learning process. The children should never feel dumb or inferior for asking any type of question. Letting the players teach each other is beneficial on many different levels when it comes to development. Later in the book in Key Point #4, I speak about "Self Organized Learning Environments"; this method or strategy for learning is excellent when it comes to teaching players how to take control of their own learning.

When it comes to learning how to become part of a team, children will benefit from even the simple things. Take for example sitting together in a pre-planned formation or shape, quieting down together in order to listen to the coach, taking one knee when the coach is talking, wearing your teams uniform or practice clothes, doing exercises together in synchronization and showing up on time for games or training. Those are some basic things that will help your child understand what being part of a team requires. However, it is up to the coach to create an

environment where the players will develop these collective skills.

1) Players want to take responsibility for their own learning.
2) Players are encouraged to adapt and build a growth mindset - striving to know more, experimenting and sharing knowledge.
3) Players should want ownership over their development as their intrinsic motivation and commitment goes up. Positive affirmations when training are encouraged.
4) Less talking by coaches and more problem-solving & learning by players.
5) The focus is on progress, getting better and learning as a group. It is never on winning.

Ideal Learning Environment For Children's Training
Performance not based on just physical qualities
Environment safe and supportive and positive
Team Unity built – encouragement
Emotional control
Group learning encourages individual learning

3

The Importance of A Qualified Coach

Let me cut right to the point. In order to become highly skilled in a particular sport a player needs instruction from a highly qualified coach.   Training with top-level players will help in their development but players need feedback and instruction from an excellent coach. I understand that it may be very difficult to find a high level coach or the cost may be too much, but eventually in order to excel a player must have access to a high level coach. If finding a qualified coach is not possible, get creative and hire a skilled high school player or college player to tutor your child. If getting any type of coach is not possible, try using the Internet with resources like "Youtube" that can provide high quality instructional content. Becoming highly skilled in a particular area is not a new concept. There has been a lot written about how the top experts in many fields have become so talented and accomplished. One of the most common themes is the presence of a highly qualified master coach. I can't stress enough how important excellent feedback is in order to progress, especially in a sport.

I worked on a golf course from the age of 16 to 23 years old. Week after week I would watch the same golfers hit the ball poorly using the same interesting swings. For the life of me I couldn't understand how people could go out and make the same mistakes over and over again for years. I wanted to play golf myself but I realized I was not great, so I decided to take a lesson. That one lesson taught me how to turn my hips and take a proper backswing. As a result, I turned into a "13" handicap golfer pretty quickly. Once I was a 13 handicap my scores didn't improve, but I didn't really put any effort into my game at that point. I am sure that if I had taken more lessons and played more, my handicap would have been much lower. I had similar experiences in other sports as well. In hindsight what I had developed was an ability to understand how to breakdown techniques and learn skills very quickly with the help of a quality coach. My main sport was soccer and I can still recall the influences top coaches had on me in the all the different aspects of my game. I can tell you exactly what I learned from each coach and top player that mentored me. In order to play at a high level it would be very beneficial to have a top coach.

#4

Utilizing The Concepts of Self-Organized Learning Environments

The below information on SOLE learning can be adapted and adjusted to fit your child's own unique situation. If you and your child wanted to use SOLE learning together to become proficient at a particular sport you could quite easily. Even though it is meant for group learning it will work well without a group setting. The concept and purpose of SOLE learning is to give children the tools to empower their own learning. They will learn to answer and eventually ask the "big" important questions, they will gain confidence through their achievements and mentor's encouragement, no question is ever seen as non-intelligent or not important, the use of the internet as a resource is critical and peer learning & teaching skills are developed and required.

Let me give you a quick example of how Self Organized Learning Environments can be used with a parent and child in the context of learning a sport. The parent would ask the child "can you show me three ways to pass a soccer ball?" The child would use the Internet to begin the research on Google, Youtube, Vimeo or similar websites. The parent would simply give positive encouragement to the child through the learning process saying things like, "I am so impressed with you, I was not as smart as you at your age!" If the child came up with the answers and it was not quite enough – the parent might say "that is really, really good work and I am very impressed but can you go a little deeper and see if you can give me a little more information". Once the child found out three ways to pass the soccer ball it would be time to go outside and practice the three passes. After practicing the passes the child would then teach the parent how make the passes. Like I mentioned most SOLE learning is done in a larger group setting but working in a small group or by individuals will bring about success as well. The SOLE learning outline below covers the major concepts of group SOLE learning. Remember almost all highly skilled experts had a mentor who provided them positive feedback, guidance and encouragement when they were learning their craft. The SOLE concept stresses positive feedback and encouragement while empowering children to take charge of their own learning. If children get positive encouragement and positive feedback while learning a sport, they will feel great about themselves while engaging in that sport. If the child feels confident they will have high self-esteem, high self-worth and associate their participation in the sport with success and enjoyment. These are some of the reasons I feel using SOLE's are so important in your child's sports development and overall development.

What is a SOLE & How Does it Work?

The concept of self-organized learning environments was invented by Dr. Sugatra Mitra, a physicist and educational researcher. The concept started out as something called "minimally invasive learning" but now it is referred to as a SOLE. SOLE learning <u>requires children to organize themselves and structure their own learning.</u> <u>using external resources usually the internet.</u>

Basics of SOLE Learning Today:

- Children should be put into teams of 4-5 students each. It is beneficial to have a few teams working in a room together so that they can share ideas and knowledge.

- Each team should have one "captain" or "team leader" who is in charge of keeping order in the group. Allowing all members to contribute and collaborate.

- Each team should have access to one computer preferably with a widescreen monitor.

- Children that are computer savvy can start working right away on the given task. If they have no computer experience then some of the earlier time is spent figuring out how to use the computer. One of Dr. Mitra's first experiments involved putting a computer in the wall of a slum in India to see how quickly the children in that neighborhood would pick up basic computer skills. Not only did these children lack computer skills, they didn't speak English; yet, they not only figured out how to use the computer, they taught themselves and others English.

- Children should be allowed to switch to another team at any time (trade).

- Children can attempt to recruit any student to join their team that they want but it must be a trade with another group to keep group numbers even.

- <u>The groups are given a question by the teacher and asked to "go find the answer". The students are not guided or coached after that point. They are just given encouragement from a mentor/teacher, internet access and the members of their group to work with.</u>

- Children can go over to other teams to observe what they are working on. They should not feel competitive with the other teams. Rather it should be seen as a positive thing to make sure the entire class succeeds.

- After a set amount of time the groups will present their results to the class as a whole.

Role of the Teacher/Mentor in a SOLE

The role of the teacher is to offer encouragement and praise, for example saying things like "you worked very hard", "I am so impressed with you" or "I didn't know that at your age"; "I am very impressed you found that out". When running a S.O.L.E there is no such thing as a bad question from a student. All students must feel free and be encouraged to ask as many questions as possible of the teacher or each other. However, the teacher should never directly answer the child's question with the final answer. Teachers will ask the children to dig a little deeper or ask them if they can look in a different place to find out more information. If the children are stuck and need a hint, the teacher can give one but it is better if the teacher says something like, "I am here for you to help in anyway, but my hope is you can do as much as this on your own with your group".

It was also found that when children were offered "easy" compared to "hard" questions, they tend to choose the "easy" questions if they were alone. However, teams or groups were more inclined to choose the "hard" questions. Lastly, using one-computer per/group forces kids to share, collaborate, communicate and come up with their own rules and roles. Collaboration is one of the cornerstones of why this teamwork works.

In order to effectively teach the kids a sport using SOLES, coaches would have to ask the important "Big Questions". Asking the "Big Questions" requires some knowledge, so students would be following a logical developmental path. A soccer coach might ask questions like "What is a 1v1 move and why would you want to learn them?" "What can my teammates do when I have the ball and need a person to pass the ball to?" or "What is does shielding the soccer ball mean in soccer and what are the important things to know about shielding the ball?"

SOLEs in Action: Case Study Examples

The examples are numerous but let me give you just a few that demonstrate the positive impact of S.O.L.Es to date:

- *The impact of access:* An underperforming class in the slums of India, knowing no English was able to raise its academic tests scores from failing to passing. The class raised its scores so high that they actually matched the scores of their peers at one of the richest highest performing schools in India.

- *The power of discovery*: 6 year old children learned to search the internet on a free computer set-up in a communal area on a street in their neighborhood, after learning how to use the computer, they eventually used their new internet skills to improve their overall academic performance in school.

- *The benefits of collaboration*: Italian students with no previous exposure to English were placed into teams and asked to find the correct answers to difficult questions written on the board in only English with no instructions. Teams were encouraged to share and collaborate, eventually all teams had developed their own unique solutions/answers to each question.

The benefits of S.O.L.Es are quite remarkable and there are many examples of S.O.L.E's in action on YouTube, I would encourage you to look them up as well as the talks by Dr. Mitra (Ted Talks). Watching the S.O.L.E's in action and listening to Dr. Mitra should help you grasp the concept even better. There is no doubt in my mind that SOLE learning will help a child excel in sports and other areas.

#5

Rapid Skill Acquisition - BDNF, Dopamine & Chunking

Learning is not easy; it requires high levels of focus, concentration, commitment, emotional control, hard work and patience. There are two chemicals in the brain that are proven to enhance the ability to learn. The first chemical in the brain that helps stimulate learning and motivation is called dopamine. The chemical "*Dopamine*" is released by the brain whenever experiences are challenging and have novelty (new experiences). When dopamine is released it creates a *sweet spot for optimal learning* to occur. Pep Guardiola (famous soccer professional soccer coach) would constantly push his players to play on the edge of their technical ability, while using diverse ever-changing training environments. By constantly adding variations to trainings, Guardiola was creating an environment for "optimum sweet spot learning", novelty was always present which made training challenging and interesting. I recently watched Guardiola running training session and noticed the players playing a juggling 1-touch game into garbage cans. Imagine Bayern playing problem-solving games into garbage cans! Novelty & Dopamine at Bayern! How does this relate to you and your child? When you are practicing, just make sure things are interesting every single day. Try creating different, fun, creative and challenging practice exercises. Make sure the training is challenging, meaning not to easy and not to hard. Children must have some success and feel challenged all at the same time. Remember in the end the major key is that the child is having lots of fun!

If the training is to easy the child will be bored. If the training is to hard they will be frustrated and want to quit. However, get the balance just right and the child will feel successful, challenged, empowered and motivated. The next chemical in the brain found to have an impact on learning is called *BDNF* or Brain-Derived Neurotropic Factor. BDNF is very important in the learning process in terms of transferring learned skills into the long-term memory. Increased BDNF levels are proven to increase learning potential. The optimal learning environment for learning new skills that can be transferred to the long-term memory is training at lower intensity levels (below 70% Maximum Heart Rate) with discontinuous training. *It is proven that learning complex things while working at physically high intensity levels (above 70% MHR) is ineffective.* The best way to make use of BDNF is by learning skills *at below 70% MRH* or right after higher intensity bursts of exercise.

The roles of Dopamine and BDNF also share many similarities with the concept of "Deliberate Practice". Anders Ericsson, a Professor of Psychology at Florida State University is a leading expert in an area called Deliberate Practice. Anders has found that becoming highly skilled in a field has more to do with how one practices compared to just the number of repetitions a person performs. Meaningful deliberate practice should not be easy or take little mental effort; deliberate practice requires hard work (*mental bandwidth*), concentration and focus. Anders also concluded that many highly skilled people tend to break down the skills being learned into *smaller chunks* while getting *feedback from a master coach*. Deliberate practice also focuses on continuously training the learned skill at more and more *challenging levels* (building neural pathways). *Working from simple to complex* is essential in the learning progression. In the context of soccer training we can use the example of learning a 1 v 1 attacking move; the initial stage would be learning the move at a very slow rate of speed and gradually increasing the speed of execution with training. Adding a defender when practicing the skill would not be introduced until after many hours of training without pressure or if the skill could be used proficiently without pressure. During the learning process the use of a master coach that provides feedback will increase the effectiveness of learning as well. Cones would be used as *visual cues and spatial indicators* for the player to execute the technique. The cones force players to figure our *space, timing, speed and proper angles*. The theory of "Deliberate Practice" is based off of the observations of highly skilled experts in all different types of fields. There is little question that "Deliberate Practice" when done correctly challenges the brain and enhances cognitive development and skill development. However, when training children you must remember they are not adults or teenagers. They need to enjoy themselves, no overtraining, no over-coaching and no pressure to win!

Rapid Skill Acquisition

Terminology

All sports require excellent technique and a wide range of skills. There is a science to teaching skills so players can literally hard wire the skills into their brain and body.

Skill – is a specific goal directed activity or movement. It can be trained and conditioned.

Cognitive skills – This is the thought process behind executing actions/skills. It is the blueprint of how to perform the skill or movement and the strategy behind executing the skill (the when and how and where to perform it)

Perceptual skills – ability to correct and adapt the skill to make it work while doing it (this is enhanced in creative cognitive exercises).

Kinesthetic – feedback you get back when performing skill.

Learning Stages

Cognitive – person has mental image of skill – key points of skill they can visualize

Associative stage – fine tuning skill and learning through trial and error

Automatous stage – can just play and not think – automatic performance of skills

Part practice or chunking – breakdown skill and train in small amounts but it will be a bit of the whole. I recommend chunking highly. This is critical if you want your child to have top-level technique. Break the skill down and perfect every part of the skill.

Whole practice – training the skill in one motion – this comes after learning the parts and chunking. Whole practice can be done at different speeds and with no pressure, passive pressure, more pressure and full pressure. Increase the intensity, speed and pressure as the player's skill level increases with the particular skill.

Strategic understanding – Learning how, when and where to use the skill – all this need to happen in split second. Top players with a wider skill range have more solutions to problems on the field.

Rapid Skill Acquisition Success Formula

1) *Deconstruct the skill* – break the skill down into its component parts. Teach he child how to deconstruct skills. This will help them when learning new skills.

2) *Practice in increments* - one increment at a time

 3) *Make skill training challenging* – practice the skill in more challenging environments

4) *Immerse yourself in the skill* – instead of training the skill 1 day a week, train the skill 5 straight days (total immersion). Total immersion is more effective in learning new skills. Total focus on the skill.

5) *Self-correction* – this is a big part of the process. Always look to self-correct the skill. Have a vivid picture of what the skill should look like, feel the skill, see the skill and perform the skill. If something is off make corrections. You may have to re-visit the fundamentals and go back to chunking and breaking down the skill into small pieces.

Why Does It Work?

"Rapid Skill Acquisition" using a large number of repetitions with total immersion will be more effective in building engrams in the player's brains. This means that skills will be stored in the long-term memory of the player as the brain is literally hard wired building neural pathways. The skill should start to become automatic as it leaves the short-term memory and is placed into the long-term memory. Having an understanding of how skills are learned and engrained in the body and brain is very important for coaches and parents. It is not good enough anymore to say go practice. The players should be educated on exactly how to practice. Bruce Lee the famous martial artist would often say "I can get more out of 3 minutes of practice than most people can get out of 3 hours." He was trying to emphasize the importance of deliberate focused practice compared to just practicing without a real purpose.

6

Have An Overall Cognitive Development Plan

Before getting into how the brain works while playing sports, it is important to grasp a general understanding of cognitive development and the human brain. The definition of cognition dates back to the 15th century meaning "thinking and awareness". Cognition is essentially the "processing of information". This includes things like calculating, reasoning, problem solving and decision-making. The processes of cognition are handled in the brain. Fields like neuropsychology and cognitive science study these processes in detail. When I mention developing a player's cognitive sports ability, I literally mean developing the player's ability to make better and quicker decisions, utilizing and recognizing important information while discarding the irrelevant information, gaining the ability to chunk information together quickly in order to make split second decisions, having the ability to consistently judge space and time correctly on the field, being able read cues in order to anticipate and problem solve on the field while creating an overall more intelligent athlete. The end result of cognitive training will be a better overall team and individual performance on the field. Individually players will see the benefits of cognitive training in their ability to concentrate, learn, focus and problem solve, not just on the field but in other areas outside of sports as well. The player's _mental bandwidth_ or ability to learn & concentrate on multiple things with efficiency will be increased. Players should begin to train better in practice after they are exposed to the cognitive training. There is also a clear and proven transfer of intelligence that will happen when players are involved in cognitive training. When a person increases their cognitive ability in one area, it will transfer to other areas. Players literally become better all-around learners across the board, which parents and teachers will be more than pleased to hear. This is why I stress the importance of implementing a well-rounded curriculum off the field for players cognitive development needs. It is vital that the brain continue to be challenged when not playing sports. The curriculum can include a variety of different activities that will increase brain plasticity.

To fully understand the "transfer of intelligence" we need to look at the make-up of intelligence. Intelligence is defined in two separate ways, crystallized intelligence and fluid intelligence. *Crystallized intelligence* is the ability to use information, skills and knowledge to score well on standardized test. This type of knowledge represents your lifetime of cerebral knowledge. Games like Jeopardy or Trivial Pursuit test a person's crystallized intelligence. Crystallized intelligence will not help players in sports in terms of decision-making and problem solving. However, the second type of intelligence called *"Fluid Intelligence"* will help players in their sports developmental process. Fluid intelligence is the ability to think logically, learn new skills and then use the knowledge gained as a platform to solve nonrelated new problems or learn new skills. The fact that fluid intelligence can be transferred and used in other related and unrelated tasks is a major break though as well. The other positive with fluid intelligence is that it can be trained and increased. The more you train your fluid intelligence the more progress and overall cognitive development increases. Increasing fluid intelligence can literally make people smarter in all areas of their lives. When humans are actively training their brain and learning they are creating new synaptic connections. These connections build on each other, creating increased neural activity and more connections. As this happens, learning is happening. The term *neural plasticity* refers to the number of connections between the *neurons* in the brain. An increase in plasticity will enhance a person's ability to learn and retain knowledge. Cognitive sports training combined with a cognitive centered lifestyle will increase a person's fluid intelligence level. Increasing fluid intelligence helps hard wire the person's brain for success by building efficient neurological pathways. Elite sports players are proven to be some of the best problem solvers on and off the field. High-level soccer players test in the top percentiles on written tests that have nothing to do with soccer compared to non-elite players and the general public. A study in Europe recently showed top goal scorers were better problem solvers than most of their teammates. That fact alone indicates that sports in general is much more of a cognitive process than most people realize. Think about this statement: "top players come up with more solutions to problems and quicker solutions to problems on the field then average players". Top players also have superior technical ability that allows them to execute skills at high rates of speed, making their problem solving and advanced anticipation skills even more effective. Lower level players are slower in the entire process of problem solving and executing their technical skills.

Lower level players often get stuck in the process of problem solving and executing while elite players will be able to come up with solutions instantly.

The military came up with the term *"Cognitive Readiness".* It means the person is in a conscious state, aware, focused and ready to learn. Preparing players both mentally and physically for training is imperative. There are a number of other controllable factors that will affect a person's ability to learn as well. These factors include proper nutrition, amount of sleep, exercise, listening to music, exposure too new challenges, environment or domain conditions, playing video games, studying academic subjects, creating art and much more. These factors and many others have been scientifically proven to enhance cognitive ability. Here are a few examples: Eating nuts and beans through out the day can help keep glucose levels in the blood steady, this helps the brain function more efficiently. How many of our players come to training who skipped lunch or ate just candy or processed foods? How many players might have stayed up late at night playing FIFA on the Xbox? It is proven that consistent and ample sleep is required to keep the brain and body functioning at a high level. Music can stimulate brain activity, enhance motor skill development and elevate training and game performance levels. Learning can even be affected by colors or the physical layout of a room. It might sound small but the set-up of the field (looking professional), players dressed in team uniforms and proper training gear or music playing during small-sided games may make a difference in learning.

Once a person understands what positive changes they can adopt into their daily lifestyle, it is up to them to incorporate these changes. Developing regular patterns and routines in life are critical in order to achieve success & consistency. When you maintain consistent routines, forming positive & productive habits are much easier. It is hard to be your best if you don't get enough rest, eat poorly, drink to much alcohol and form unhealthy relationships. **Developing your player's cognitive abilities and forming positive lifestyle habits should not happen solely on the sports field.** Every coaching situation is different, but at the very least providing your players with positive lifestyle guidelines will be helpful. Parents should encourage their children to take part in new activities like calligraphy, playing an instrument, studying academics, taking a museum tour, playing Sudoku, reading maps, creating art or playing some challenging video games. All these activities will increase their overall cognitive ability, in turn making them better learners and players! In ancient times the "Samurai" would study gardening, landscaping, poetry, the tea ceremony and calligraphy to open up their minds. They would study the arts of peace with the left hand and the arts of war with the right hand. Another great way to increase cognitive ability is to force your self to figure things out without the use of technology on a daily basis. Instead of using a GPS, map the directions out yourself. Put away the calculator and solve problems with a pencil and paper. The more you make your brainwork to solve every day problems the more cognitive development and fluid intelligence will increase. Technology does of course come with many benefits. It allows us to experience other cultures with just a few clicks on the keyboard. Gaining insight and perspective into other cultures, societies and people can open up our minds to new ideas and ways of thinking as well. Exposure to outside cultures and other ways of life allows us to see different perspectives. These unique and different perspectives can stimulate our brains and enhance our cognitive development. Exposure to outside influences can create an appreciation for others, bring about compassion, help us develop understanding, help give us perspective and spark new ideas. Learning and cognitive development is about exposing ourselves to new things that will help us ultimately become more intelligent and well-rounded people. *In order to keep the brain constantly working and progressing, once you learn a new skill move on to the next thing to keep the brain challenged. Efficiency is not the brains friend when trying to learn.* We can then hopefully transfer that intelligence into many other areas of life, making a positive long lasting impact on society. All that may sound a little removed from the sports arena, but the reality is everything is connected. Developing an overall cognitive development plan for children off the field will benefit them on the field and in life as well. Overall cognitive development is a win/win situation for every one involved. As the world changes we must change. 65% of the jobs elementary school kids will eventually fill don't even exist yet. If you told a person in 1983 they would work as a social media consultant, they would have been confused because social media didn't even exist in 1983. The point is the best thing we can ever do is to develop our cognitive abilities, because our ability to transfer knowledge and learn can be used to succeed not just on the field, but in a changing world as well.

14 THINGS YOU CAN DO TO GET SMARTER & LIVE A COGNITIVE CENTERED LIFESTYLE SUMMARY

1) Keep Blood Sugar Levels Consistent: Fluctuation's in blood sugar levels can effect the brain. Eat small snacks throughout the day to keep thinks in check and your brain running well.

2) Play A Few Video Games: People who play video games have more brain cells. The more brain cells the better your ability to learn. Keep changing the games you play to force the brain to adjust and problem solve.

3) Watch Less TV: People who watch too much TV show lower mental acuity scores than those who watched less. ADHD is more common in people who watch more TV than those who do not.

4) Exercise: Consistent physical activity helps slow or possibly reverse the brain's physical breakdown over the years. Exercise allows your brain to function better.

5) Eat Fish: Eating fish can increase certain types of intelligence.

6) Quit Smoking: Tobacco decreases mental performance and overall brain function.

7) Drink Coffee: Coffee can increase the strength of electrical brain signals and make you more alert.

8) Hydrate: Dehydration can shrink your brain and instantly decrease the brains ability to function.

9) Positive Thoughts – What you think can lead to what you are or how you will do.

10) Learn a New Skill: Challenging your brain to always be learning new things will develop new connections in the brain. Intelligence in one area can be transferred into other areas so learning a new skill will be helpful!

11) Listen to Music: Learning to play an instrument is the best for your brain but even listening to music can help develop the brain.

12) Practice Memorizing Random Things: Think of this as a practical tune up for your brain.

13) Get Your Sleep: Get your eight hours per/night and your brain will work better. Cheat yourself on sleep and your brain will struggle to perform at a high level.

14) No Stress: Stress harms the body and brain. Effective stress management tools are essential for brain functioning and health.

QUICK BRAIN FACTS

- The brain is a 3 lb. super-computer
- 75% of the brain is made-up of water
- There are 100,000 miles of blood vessels in the brain
- The brain uses 20% of the total oxygen in the body and almost 1/3 of our calories
- The Brain has 86 billion neurons in it.
- Uses 500 calories per/day for energy
- Information can be processed at 268 mph in the brain
- Your daily habits can accelerate or decelerate brain aging
- Sports that involve hard head contact can damage the brain permanently
- When the body becomes dehydrated the brains ability to function severely decreases. In sports "stay hydrated" to stay focused!
- Drugs and alcohol use can damage the brain permanently
- Obesity can damage the brain structure, shrink the brain and reduce brain function. Obesity is not your brains friend. This is proven.
- Smoking decreases blood flow to the brain and will damage the brain
- Negative Thoughts will hurt the brain
- Environmental toxins damage the brain
- The food you eat can kill or heal you and your brain
- Maintaining a healthy diet that is free of harmful toxic food is essential for a healthy brain. Brain scans over the past 30 years prove this.
- 8 hours sleep per/night is needed. Less sleep will mean less blood flow to the brain and increase in hunger. Being tired and not well rested can lead to obesity and decreased brain function.
- Living a healthy lifestyle can improve brain health in as little as two months.

7

Play As Much As You Can. Best vs. Best?

If you want your child to excel in a sport you must provide an opportunity for them to play outside of their regular practice. At the famous soccer club in Holland called "Ajax FC" they have a soccer fun park for the youth players. The kids go on the weekends and play soccer volleyball, soccer tennis, futsal and much more. There is no coach to instruct them during this time and the children are free to choose whatever soccer variation they want to play at the park. This type of non-structured play is very important in a child's development. Children need time to just play and try everything they learned from training without the coach present. Playing so called "street ball" gives kids a chance to play without fear and lets them really express themselves on the field. One of my friends has three sons under the age of 10 who all play soccer. He converted his front yard into a 5v5 soccer field with real goals. All the kids from the neighborhood come by and play the minute school is out. They play these pick up games every day until the sun goes down. It is no coincidence that my friend's sons are already very skilled at such a young age. They play all the time and their dad was a good player who taught them technique. They had a combination of street soccer (their front yard), club soccer and their dad teaching them. The result is a winning combination for his boys. This situation is essentially a formula for success that their parents helped create for them.

Another example of an athlete who became an incredible professional is "Pistol Pete" Marovich. He was one of first special technical and creative basketball players of his time period. He did things with a basketball that were never seen before and technically far superior and creative compared to anyone else in the game. After reading the story about his life, one major thing stuck out to me. "Pistol" was obsessed and never went anywhere without his basketball. Even in the movie theatre he would be sitting and bouncing the ball, taking little dribbling touches with both hands. That type of commitment and total immersion is part of what made the ball an extension of the body. The ball never left his finger-tips, on or off the court! Pistol Pete understood that in order to be the best his dedication needed to be higher than anyone else. Many of the greats have very similar stories!

Let's look at another example involving elite table tennis players in the UK. Table tennis takes some physical ability but much more eye hand coordination, technical ability and strategy than anything else. Interestingly enough, the vast majority of the UK's best table tennis players come from the same tiny town in Reading, England. In fact, they come from the same tiny street in Reading. How is this possible? Is there something in the water? There must be an explanation why so many tennis table champions are from Reading, England? There is an explanation and it makes perfect sense. One of the best table tennis coaches in the country built a small outside table tennis garage on his property. He opened the garage up for all the local players to use. <u>The coach also gave every player a set of keys to the garage so players could play 24 hours a day if they wished. Because there were so many</u>

good players using the garage, players were always playing against the best competition. The players also had the benefit of expert feedback from a top-level coach and other top-level players. The environment was perfect for players who treated table tennis almost like an obsession.

There are many more examples of small unassuming training centers that produce highly skilled experts around the world. The book *The Talent Code* talks about a tiny tennis school in Russia that produces more top-level tennis players than the entire United States. There is a famous small music school in Dallas that produces some of the world's top musicians, mostly attributed to the fact that the teachers encourage the students to breakdown their music practice in small pieces, and practice at slow speeds. At the school there is a popular joke that if someone is walking by the school and can recognize the song that is being played, the students are playing it to fast. *The Talent Code* makes the important point that whatever you are trying to learn you must have many meaningful repetitions. Playing against the best players possible will give players the meaningful training they need to excel. However, at what age should players play against the best? My opinion is that young players should learn quality technique and worry less about playing against the best players. It is an added bonus to grow up playing against other top players and there is no doubt they will learn from each other. I just do not like the idea of separating players to early for the reasons I have explained earlier. At 13 years old the select teams, all-stars, regional teams or whatever you want to call them can be formed. Don't worry about best vs. best until your child is turning 13 years old.

8

Sports Specialization or Diversity?

In order to become a top athlete does a child need to specialize in one sport at a very young age? My answer is simple. No! Children will benefit greatly by participating in a wide variety of sports and activities. Spatial awareness, body awareness, agility, balance, eye hand coordination and much more will be better developed with a variety of activities. One of the most advanced soccer training centers in the world is located in the country of Qatar. The center wanted a curriculum for the young players, so they asked one of the worlds leading experts to help design a custom curriculum. He immediately suggested a curriculum that included a wide variety of sports. He stressed a diverse sporting experience in order to develop spatial awareness and an understanding of movement, angles and timing in spaces. Specialization is something that can start around 13 years old.

If your child shows a real interest in a particular sport than of course you may want to do more for them in that sport. Tiger Woods would watch golf videos non-stop since he was tiny child. His dad was a golfer and he loved golf from the time he was an infant. I am sure his parents offered him opportunities at an early age to explore his interest in the game and pursue it. The key is that training extra in a sport is the child's choice not the coaches or parents. The children must be having fun with the extra training and want to be there. Once an athlete is in their teens they must realize in order to make a top level it require lots of sacrifice and hard work. Some training days will not be as fun as others and rest assured there will be some struggles. One of the top martial arts teachers in the world said, "in order to become highly skilled the student must be able to taste bitter". Behind every great performance is a lifetime of hard work and hard work can be just that – "Hard and Bitter at Times!"

List of Sources

1. *The Talent Code…* by Daniel Coyle. Published by Bantam Book May 2009

2. *Practice Perfect…* by Doug Lemov,Erica Woolway & Katie Yezzi… Published by Jossey-Bass.. 2012

3. *Outliers…* by Malcolm Gladwell… Published by Little Brown and Company… 2s008

4. *Bounce…*by Mathew Syed.. Published by Harper Perenial.. 2011

5. *Flow…* by Mihaly Csikszentmihalyi…Published by Harper Collins…1990.